About the Book

In this book we visit a country that has undergone more changes in the past 30 years than in all the centuries before. It's a land where camel herds graze along one of the world's longest oil pipelines. It's a place where a railroad train makes stops in a flourishing oasis city. It's a region where asphalt highways cut across the desert sand like strips of black ribbon.

What has brought about these striking contrasts? The story goes back to 1938 when oil was discovered in the Saudi desert. From then on progress has been the order of the day in Saudi Arabia. The income from oil has enabled the people to irrigate their arid lands, build schools and create electric power. It has given a fabled land a fabulous future.

We see much of this development through the eyes of Hassan (whose name means Good) and his sister Karima (Generous) and learn what happens when their Bedouin cousin comes to town! These children, like other Saudis in this book, are the author's friends and when we finish reading it, they are also ours.

About the Illustrator

HARIS PETIE, who studied under Norman Rockwell in Paris, is equally at home with nations and children. Mother of two, this widely traveled, long-time illustrator of children's books has illustrated eleven *Getting to Know* books with a grace which grows from respect for readers and text.

About the Author

On TED PHILLIPS' most recent visit to Saudi Arabia, he was stopped on the street of Al Khobar by a boy with a brand-new camera slung over his flowing white robe. "May I take your picture in color?" the youngster asked in perfect English. The author, who, during his 20 years of several-times-a-year trips to Saudi Arabia, has taken many pictures of the Saudis in their elaborate costumes, was somewhat astounded to have the tables turned.

For the most part, however, he expects such changes in Saudi Arabia, which he has come to know through his association with the oil industry. Previously a reporter for Associated Press, he is well equipped to convey to us his understanding of his Saudi friends. When not with them, Ted Phillips lives in Goldens Bridge, New York.

About the Getting to Know Series

This round-the-world series not only covers everyday life in many countries and regions and includes their geography and history — it also highlights *what's new today*. The series offers timely — and often first — reports on the birth of new nations in Africa and Asia, the splitting of ancient nations like China, the let's-get-together movement of members of Europe's and Latin America's Common Markets, and the struggles of two-thirds of the world to attain the good life possessed by the other third. *To keep each book up to date in these fast-changing times, it is revised with every new printing.*

Specific countries in the *Getting to Know* series are determined by a survey of curriculum specialists in the fifty states. Made every two years, the survey is used to relate GTK subject matter to classroom needs. To insure intimacy as well as immediacy, authors are chosen first of all for the quality of their personal experience with the subject matter. All *Getting to Knows* are also checked by experts prior to publication.

Getting to Know

SAUDI ARABIA

by
TED PHILLIPS

illustrated by HARIS PETIE

Coward, McCann & Geoghegan, Inc.
New York

To Mother, Ned, Jane, Steve, Alfred and Brown

Library of Congress Catalog Card Number: 63-15550

Editor of this series: Sabra Holbrook

MANUFACTURED IN THE UNITED STATES OF AMERICA

NINTH IMPRESSION, REVISED 1973

The ancient camel caravan routes that were once the tradeways of Arabia have almost disappeared. The camel is still the way to travel for some desert families, but traders prefer paved highways, railroads and jet air lanes. Each year the desert kingdom of Saudi Arabia takes more giant steps toward becoming a modern nation.

In this book you will see the country changing before your eyes.

Look first at the map. It shows that Saudi Arabia takes up most of the Arabian Peninsula, in the southwestern corner of the continent of Asia. Like huge arms, famous bodies of water hug the country. On the west lies the long, narrow Red Sea. The warm waters of the Persian Gulf* wash the east coast. To the south is Arabian Sea.

* Also referred to as the Arabian Gulf.

Saudi Arabia has many neighbors. Some of them are large and some are very small. Jordan, Iraq and the tiny state of Kuwait are on the north. Yemen and the Peoples Democratic Republic of Southern Yemen fit into the southwest corner of the peninsula like little pieces of a jigsaw puzzle. Qatar sticks out like a thumb into the Persian Gulf. The southeast corner is made up of the Sultanate of Oman, including the district of Dhufar and the Union of the Arab Amirates.

Saudi Arabia occupies all but about 130,000 of the Arabian Peninsula's million or so square miles. It's nearly one-third the size of the United States. A little over four and a half million people, almost half the population of the peninsula, live in Saudi Arabia.

If you were to fly westward across the country from the new international airport at Dhahran, on the Persian Gulf, you could watch dramatically changing scenes unfold below you.

After leaving the Gulf, you see rolling plains, with some bushes and grass; then the bush and grass give way to gravel. Just beyond, the earth begins to ripple with waves of sand dunes, and beyond the dunes rise rocky plateaus. The plateaus stretch 300 miles to mountains which reach up and up—from 4,000 to 8,000 feet. Bare of any trees or vegetation, these mountains rise from the sand like fairy-tale castles.

After crossing them, you land at Jiddah, once again in a flat area, on the shore of the Red Sea. Now you have an aerial picture of Saudi Arabia.

The father of this desert country was King Abd al-Aziz ibn Abd al-Rahman Al Faisal Al Saud. For short, he was called King Ibn Saud, which means "Son of Saud." You can see that the country was named after the royal family. Saudi Arabs are often called Saudis. Theirs is one of the few non-constitutional monarchies in the world. Saudi Arabia has a Consultative Assembly which helps pass the laws, but it is responsible to the King rather than to the people. The King and his cabinet make the final decisions.

King Ibn Saud was born in 1880 and was a great warrior by the time he was twenty years old. He grew to be a big man, six feet four inches tall, and weighing 260 pounds. He made an impressive figure riding across the desert on his black Arabian stallion. His body carried many scars of battle, which showed he fought up front with his men. By 1920, after 25 years of fierce battles, he had made a united country out of a group of warring tribes. It was then that he was proclaimed King.

King Ibn Saud died in 1953, and his eldest son, Saud ibn Abd al-Aziz, became King for a while. In 1964 another of Ibn Saud's sons became King. He was Faisal ibn Abd al-Aziz, who had often served as one of Saudi Arabia's delegates to the United Nations. When this world organization was founded in 1945, the country became a charter member.

KING
IBN SAUD

Faisal, who last visited the United States in 1971, had learned much abroad. He worked hard to move Saudi Arabia ahead. For centuries the people had been very poor. There are still some very poor people in Saudi Arabia, as there are anywhere and particularly in the less-developed countries of the world. But a great deal is being done to get rid of poverty in Saudi Arabia. And it is being done in a hurry.

In recent years the Saudi Arab government has built schools, hospitals, highways and seaports. It has started irrigation projects to give the farmers more water for their crops of barley, wheat, alfalfa, coffee, fruit and vegetables. It has set aside money to take care of old and sick people. Once many Saudi Arabians suffered from malaria, a disease carried by the anopheles mosquito. Today there are fewer mosquitoes in the country and much less malaria. A government spraying program is getting rid of the pests.

The Saudi Arabs are lucky to be able to pay for these improvements. They have something the whole world wants: oil. Back in 1933, King Ibn Saud signed an agreement to permit American oilmen to search for oil in his country. They found it, and today Saudi Arabia can boast of being one of the largest oil-producing countries in the world. Money from oil is what is changing the country so fast.

The people's language, however, hasn't changed much in 1,500 years. They speak Arabic, which is a Semitic tongue and is like Hebrew in many ways. With almost 80 million speakers, Arabic is one of the world's ten most widely spoken languages. It's heard more often than either French or Italian. You hear it in Morocco, near the Atlantic Ocean. You hear it in Algeria, on the Mediterranean; in parts of East Africa on the Indian Ocean.

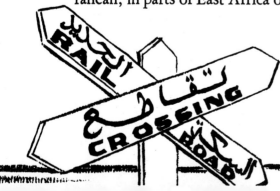

You hear it in the Sahara desert and in the bazaars of Cairo on the Nile River. You hear it in snow-covered hamlets in the hills of Lebanon and in other Middle Eastern countries that connect the Arabian Peninsula with the mainland of Asia. Each of these countries speaks the language in a slightly different way. In Saudi Arabia, the homeland of the Arabs, you hear a dialect nearest to the original classic Arabic.

The language seems difficult for Americans to learn. It has many sounds that are hard to master. Also, the words are written from right to left. In our eyes, the Arabs seem to write backward. But to them, it is we who write in the wrong direction! Arabic script, with its many curves and swirls, is beautiful to look at. When spoken, it has a remarkable lilt.

American children whose fathers are oilmen in Saudi Arabia study Arabic in school as a regular course. They have less trouble learning it than their parents, because children get used to new sounds more rapidly than grown-ups.

Our own English language has many words from Arabic. Algebra, the name of a kind of mathematics you will study in junior high school, stems from the Arabic word *al-jabr*. The name of another science you will probably take, chemistry, comes from the Arabic *al-kimiya*.

ALGEBRA

$$x - y \,)\overline{\begin{array}{l} x + y \\ x^2 + xy \\ - xy - y^2 \\ \hline x^2 - y^2 \end{array}}$$

The Arabs made many important discoveries that affect our lives today, but many historians believe that their greatest contribution was in the field of mathematics. Our present way of writing numbers came directly from the Arabs. They also introduced the zero. The word cipher, which means the same thing as zero, comes from the Arabic word *sifr*, which means empty.

The Arabs did a great deal of work in astronomy, too. Their traders sailed back and forth across the Indian Ocean to East Africa, and navigation on the sea as well as on the wide-open deserts made it necessary for them to use the stars as guideposts. Most of the stars in the heavens were named by the Arabs. For example, the name of the star Acrab means scorpion in Arabic. Algedi is Arabic for goat; Altair for eagle. Many other terms in this branch of science are also Arabic. Two common ones are zenith, the point at which the sun is directly overhead, and nadir, the point directly opposite to the zenith.

Arabs also devised many ways of detecting symptoms of sickness and fighting it with medicines made from plants and chemicals. The Arabs have been called the first druggists. Some of the remedies they perfected were syrups for coughs, balsam for healing wounds, camphor for relaxing tight muscles and borax as an antiseptic. The ancient Arabs even had regulations like ours today against selling drugs that might be harmful, without permission from a doctor.

One of the world's great religions, Islam, was born in ancient Arabia. It is the religion of the Saudi Arabs today. Islam means submission to the will of God. People of the Islamic faith are called Moslems. Islam has a good deal in common with the religions of Christians and Jews. The followers of all three believe in a single God, whom the Moslems call Allah. They obey the same Ten Commandments that we do. Moslems don't criticize other religions, although they believe theirs to be the truest. They do their best to tell other people about Islam.

Islam was founded by Mohammed almost 1,400 years ago. The Koran is the Moslem holy book. Most of it was handed down, as the word of God, by the Prophet Mohammed. Moslems often repeat, *"La ilaha illa Allah,"* which means. "There is no god, but God," and they add, "Mohammed is the messenger of God." The Saudis are reminded of this belief every time they see their flag. The saying is inscribed in Arabic on the green flag of the kingdom.

When the Saudis pray, they kneel and face Mecca, the holiest city for the world's 500,000,000 Moslems. Mecca, a Saudi Arab city near the Red Sea, is the birthplace of the Prophet Mohammed. Only people of the Moslem faith may enter the city. Airplane pilots are requested not to fly over it because the noise might disturb those at prayer. There are many praying there, for each year thousands of Moslems from all over the world make pilgrimages to Mecca. All Moslems try to make the pilgrimage at least once in their lives.

Believers in Islam must perform many other difficult duties. One of them is the fast of Ramadhan. During this month, Moslems must not eat or drink from dawn until sunset. The fast begins each day where there is enough light to tell a white thread from a black one.

Ramadhan is the ninth month in the Islamic calendar. Like ours, the calendar contains 12 months. The months of the Islamic year are called:

Muharram

Safar

Rabi' al-Awwal

Rabi' al-Thani

Jumada al-Ula

Jumada al-Akhirah or al-Thaniyah

Rajab

Sha'ban

Ramadhan

Shawwal

Dhu al-Qa'dah

Dhu al-Hijjah

Except for having 12 months, the Islamic calendar is very different from ours. It's based on the movements of the moon, while ours is based on the movements of the earth in relation to the sun. There is a new moon about every 29½ days. Since 12 times 29½ equals 354, the Islamic year has only 354 days instead of the 365 in our calendar. The last month of this calendar, Dhu al-Hijjah, is the pilgrimage month.

MEDINA

Not far from Mecca is Medina, the second holiest city of Islam. The Arabic name for Medina is al-Madinah al-Munawwarah, which means the Illuminated City. The tomb of the Prophet Mohammed is there, and it was in this city that he built the first mosque. A mosque, or *masjid*, is a Moslem church.

This first mosque was a simple square enclosure surrounded by brick and stone walls. Only a part of it had a roof, made of palm leaves, supported by wood from date trees. Later, magnificent mosques were built throughout the world, but they are all designed in the same shape as the first mosque that Mohammed built. Before a Moslem enters a mosque to pray, he always removes his shoes and washes himself with water provided for this purpose near the entrance.

Moslems are required to pray five times a day—at dawn, at midday, in late afternoon, at sunset and in the evening. They are called to prayer by the *muezzin*, who stands on a balcony near the top of a minaret, a mosque's steeple. He chants in a voice that carries far over the rooftops. He summons the people to prayer by calling: "God is great." He says this four times and then continues with other praises. At dawn, he finishes his call by saying: "Prayer is better than sleep."

Faithful Moslem pilgrims on their way to Mecca arrive by ship or plane at Jiddah, where you landed on your first flight across the country. It's one of the most important ports on the Red Sea, and a scene of great contrasts—with ancient market places, modern apartment houses and a busy airport. Jiddah is believed by some to be the place where Eve is buried. The word *jaddah* means grandmother in Arabic. The city is said to be named for the grandmother of the human race.

Nearly 600 miles inland from Jiddah, almost in the center of Saudi Arabia, is Riyadh, the civil capital of the country. The King has one of his palaces here. The other is in Mecca, which is considered the religious capital of the country. Riyadh is a city of broad-laned boulevards, divided by sections of palm trees and other greenery. The traffic cops at intersections stand under umbrella-like shelters to protect them from the sun. Into the city and around its balconied apartment houses and bright-awninged stores sweep the desert sands.

Riyadh is the last stop on the Saudi Arab Government Railroad, which starts at Dammam, a commercial port on the Persian Gulf. Dammam has one of the longest piers in the world. It stretches seven miles into the water, so that ocean-going ships may dock far out in the Persian Gulf, because the water is too shallow closer to shore. The railroad runs out to the end of the pier where the ships are loaded and unloaded.

Most of the other Saudi cities are built near an oasis, a place in the desert which is kept green by underground springs. Some of the springs produce as much as 3,000 gallons of water a minute. The water comes from deep down in the earth, often 40 or 50 feet below the surface. It's usually quite warm—80 or 90 degrees. For hundreds of years, the oasis people used donkeys to lift the water up to the surface in goatskin bags attached to ropes. Today, modern pumps have replaced the donkeys. The *ain*, as Arabs call the spring, is a favorite meeting place for friends and a picnic spot for families.

One of the most fascinating of the oasis cities is Hofuf, on the Persian Gulf. Around the city is the largest oasis in Saudi Arabia and one of the largest on earth. Until recently, the city was surrounded by walls built hundreds of years ago to keep out invaders. Now it's a stop on the SAG Railroad. SAG stands for Saudi Arab Government.

HOFUF

KANAD

In and around this city, you would have an exciting time. On a day's outing on the warm, pale, blue-green waters of the Persian Gulf, you might catch several kinds of fish. Among them are the *hamur* which resembles a sea bass, the *kanad* which is like a mackerel, and the four-foot-long *qidd*. This fish is a barracuda, something like a small shark. The *sayyafi* looks like a sawfish. Sea turtles, shrimp and dolphin also are very common. Once in a while, a whale comes close to shore.

In the city itself you would especially enjoy a visit to the *suq*, or market place. Here goods are piled high on the ground outside all the small shops and stalls. You see carved metal chests, copper coffeepots, large copper and brass trays inlaid with silver, beautiful silks and hand-woven baskets.

23

In a tiny stall a man is selling pearls. He displays them on a square piece of soft chamois. These pearls come from the Persian Gulf. The fleets of pearling ships are quite a sight as they leave port and sail far out in the Gulf. The pearl divers wear swimming trunks and nose clips that look like clothespins. They carry baskets fastened to a rope. After they have gathered the pearl oysters from the sea bottom, the baskets are pulled to the surface by the men in the boats. A diver can stay down, holding his breath, for as much as two minutes at a time. Sometimes he may go as deep as 90 feet. Usually the divers receive no wages, but share in the profits of the catch. The pearls are sold to the merchants you saw in the stall, who in turn sell them to people like your mother and father, and you when you get a little older.

The suq shopkeeper may speak a little English or none at all, but even if you don't know Arabic you can get along just fine. When two people really try, they can make each other understand

without being able to speak the same language. They use their hands and express themselves with their faces.

The storekeeper is polite and friendly. When he sees you enter, he says, "*Ahlan wa sahlan*," which means "Welcome." If you do know a little Arabic you say, "*As-salaam alaykum*," which means "Peace be upon you." He might answer you by saying, "*Wa-alaykum as-salaam*," which means, "And upon you be peace." He might also say, "*Kayf haalak?*" and you answer, "*Tayyib, ashkurak.*" He said, "How are you?" and you answered, "Fine, thank you." It's fun to say something in Arabic and have the

storekeeper understand you. After he's greeted you, he will be glad to have you look around for hours if you feel like it.

If you decide to buy something you will pay in *riyals*. The Saudi riyal, which is worth about 27 cents, is about the size of a dollar bill. Only coins were used for many years, but paper money is what one sees most of the time now. For buying things worth less than a riyal, a coin called a *qirsh* is used. One quirsh is worth about 1⅓ cents.

In another suq, in the bustling Persian Gulf city of al-Khobar, your father could buy the latest model automobile if he chose. The streets of this city are lined with air-conditioned apartment houses. Above their rooftops television antennas make a jungle of metal rods. Down a side street, away from the many noises of the

al-Khobar

busy main avenue, is a brand-new hospital with the very latest equipment.

About 90 per cent of the Saudi Arabs live in cities such as this one and in the oasis towns. The others roam the desert with their sheep and goats and camels. These wanderers are the Bedouins, which means "desert dwellers." When they come to a spot where they want to stay a while, they set up their black tents. When they reach an oasis, they sell a few of their animals for meat. Then they buy the dates and vegetables that oasis farmers raise.

The Bedouin is a hardy and self-reliant and very dignified person. He knows almost every inch of the part of the desert which he frequents the way you know your own backyard. In fact, he knows it better. Some Bedouins are famous as trackers, or desert detectives. They can track a lost camel, a lost jeep or a lost man with amazing skill and speed.

From a faint footprint in the sand, which you might not even see, these desert sleuths can describe the man who walked there. They can tell you his height and weight and almost the exact time he stepped on the sand. They always find their man. In fact, their description of a footprint is used in law courts in Saudi Arabia the way fingerprints are used in American courts.

At night, around the campfires, Bedouin fathers may tell their children exciting tales about the golden days of the Arabs and the valor and courage of the Arab warriors of long ago. One story is about Abu Zaid al-Hilali and his magic horse. That beautiful Arabian steed could fly all the way from Hofuf to Damascus and back in a single night.

Life in the desert, close to nature, holds many real adventures as exciting as these old tales. It takes great courage and skill to be able to live on the open sands day in and day out, but there's a freedom about the life of the Bedouin that few other people on earth know. To maintain it the Bedouin often relies upon his camel.

No animal has served the people of the desert in more ways than the camel. It carries Bedouins sometimes as far as 50 miles across the desert in one day, and it can transport loads as heavy as 500 pounds. It performs these feats on sand so soft that human beings flounder in it.

In Saudi Arabia the camel is the dromedary type that has one hump. (The Bactrian camels of Asia have two.) The hump is a storage place for fat. The camel can live for days on this fat when there isn't any other food. In his stomach he stores water. He can drink and store 30 gallons at one time. This storage system lets him travel long distances across the desert without eating or drinking.

Besides transportation, the camel supplies milk and meat. From camel hide the Saudis make sandals and water bags. They use camel hair to make rugs, cloth and very strong tents.

This useful animal has a rather odd look about him. When he sticks his head high in the air like a giraffe, he's about nine feet tall. His face is long and wears a sort of superior expression, but his deep brown eyes with their long eyelashes are very appealing. Like almost everything else about him, these lashes have a special purpose in the desert. They protect his eyes from sand and dust. Even

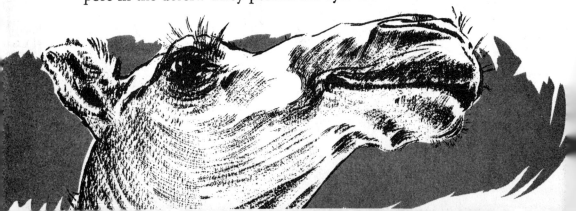

his nostrils are designed for desert living. He can shut them to slits to keep the sand out of his nose.

Maybe the Arabian animal you've heard the most about, however, is the famous Arabian horse. Although it can't really gallop as fast as in the folk tales, it's known throughout the world for its speed and beauty. But no desert animal is quite as speedy as the shy, graceful gazelle, which can step along at 50 miles an hour. It makes a wonderful pet if you find a very young one who has strayed from his mother. The gazelle loves to eat cigarettes. To be

GAZELLE

ORYX

his pal, all you have to do is give him a king-size one, but be sure it doesn't have a filter. Gazelles don't like filters.

Then there is the inquisitive hedgehog, the long-eared black goat, the sly desert fox, and the gentle oryx, which is like a large antelope. There are the saluqi dogs, too, which run amost as fast as the gazelle. Their top speed is 40 miles an hour.

One unforgettable animal in Saudi Arabia is the little donkey. You see him everywhere, loaded down with straw and sometimes with big baskets on each side. Usually, the donkey has a little bell around his neck which tinkles a merry tune as he trots along on unshod feet. At the sound of the bell, a fierce-looking lizard may scurry out of the way. Above, in the almost always blue sky, you can spot falcons, eagles, hawks and ravens. And at night you may hear the owls calling.

SWARM
OF LOCUSTS

But the Saudis could do without the locust. Millions of them fly in swarms, often hiding the sun and devouring every living green thing in sight. Some of these grasshopperlike insects get a big surprise, however. Some Bedouins roast them for dessert. Locusts are considered a delicacy in the United States, too. You can buy them in fancy grocery stores. Try one sometime. It tastes like a hazelnut.

Trees are scarce in the desert. There are no forests, but a few large trees do stand like single soldiers against the sky. The tamarisk, with fernlike branches, is often planted in rows to break the strong winds. These trees are also used to stop the sand from blowing into towns.

The most useful of all trees are the date palms of the oases. The people eat dates raw, cooked and baked into cakes. They make a delicious syrup out of them. The wood from the palms is used to build huts and the leaves for making baskets and mats.

The palms are giant trees. Some grow as tall as 80 feet. The date pickers shinny almost to the top to fill their palm-leaf baskets with big clusters of the fruit. Some trees bear dates for as long as 80 years and live to be 200 years old.

People are apt to think the desert is always bare, but this is a mistake. In March and April delicate flowers spring up in the sand. Even in the vast expanses of the worst part of the desert, millions of *zahra hamra*, which are pink orchidlike blooms, may appear.

Other beautiful desert flowers are the *dhanun* and the *barwag*. The dhanun is a solid cluster of little yellow blossoms, something like a hyacinth. When the hot sun dries it up, it looks like a long pineapple. The barwag is a white flower that looks like a lily. Fortunately for camels, many kinds of bushes dot the wide expanses of sand. The camels eat the bushes. Most of the shrubs don't have much food value, however, so a camel has to eat as much as three bushels of bushes before he's satisfied.

The camels, as well as the Bedouins' sheep and goats, also eat the grasses that appear after the winter rains. These animals especially love the bushlike *hamdh* that contains a good deal of salt. The root of a bush called *rak* serves the Bedouins as a toothbrush. Maybe something in it gives them the beautiful white teeth that shine against their tan faces.

King Ibn Saud was especially loved by the Bedouins. When he was a boy he spent a number of years living with them in the desert. The boy who was to become a king learned many things from the Bedouins which helped him later as a warrior and a diplomat.

It was he who told the Bedouins to help American oilmen learn how to live in the desert when they first came there to hunt for oil in 1933. In 1938, the oil was discovered and after World War II, operations really began to hum.

Maybe you wonder why it took so long to find the oil. The search is a difficult and expensive process. First a geologist, whom oilmen often call a "rock hound," studies the surface for clues that may tell him what's down below. Among other things, he looks for rocks and fossils. Fossils are the remains or imprints of animals or plants that lived millions of years ago. From what the rock hound finds he can tell whether the area he is searching was once under water. Most oil is found in places which ages ago were covered with water.

After the rock hounds study the surface of the earth, they bring in delicate scientific instruments to detect what lies below. They measure the pull of gravity. They test the magnetism of underground rocks. They set off explosions, and then time and measure the echoes from deep in the earth. On the basis of all these clues, they select a likely place to drill a well into deep-hidden rocks which they hope may contain a deposit of oil.

Engineers then move in a 136-foot-high derrick, equipped with a strong engine and large drilling bits. Men work in three shifts, all through the day and night, as the bit bores down into the earth. In Saudi Arabia, it usually takes less than a month to drill a well about one mile deep. This is the depth at which oil is often found there. However, once oilmen drilled 14,875 feet, or almost three miles down, and still didn't find any oil. It cost $5,000,000 to drill this "dry hole." A dry hole is a well that doesn't produce any oil. You can see that the oil business can be very risky. Big sums of money can be lost.

When a well does have oil, a "Christmas tree" is placed on its mouth. In oilmen's language, a Christmas tree means a number of crisscrossed pipes and valves or faucets which are used to control the flow of oil at the surface. After the Christmas tree is set in place, the derrick is moved away on ten or twelve huge rubber-tired wheels to begin its work all over again at another spot. Sometimes the wells are many miles apart.

The never-ending search for precious oil is still going on. It takes the exploration parties out into the waters of the Persian Gulf, for oil can be found under the bottom of the sea. Explorers also go farther and farther into the desert. They have even found their way into the mysterious Rub al-Khali, or Empty Quarter, in southern Saudi Arabia. Before oilmen entered this 250,000-square-mile region, which is as large as Texas, only a few venturesome Bedouins had ever had the courage to go into its sun-baked wasteland.

The Rub al-Khali has some of the world's highest sand dunes. These tremendous dunes are 12 miles long and 600 feet high. Here the sands have almost every color in the rainbow. They are silver, gold, brown, red and purple. The sand gets so hot—up to 165 degrees—that it would blister your feet. Nevertheless, the oilmen stay in this area as long as three months at a time. They travel and live in air-conditioned trailers, carrying their water in huge tank trucks. The food and other supplies are flown in by airplane.

About 950 American geologists, drillers and other oilmen live with their families in Saudi Arabia, mostly in Dhahran, Abqaiq and Ras Tanura. In contrast to the Empty Quarter, these towns are very pleasant places to live in. Their wide streets are lined with trees. There are tennis courts, swimming pools, movie houses, golf courses, bowling alleys and many other leisure-time attractions. Offices and homes are air-conditioned.

Usually the houses are one story high, build of cement blocks or stone from local quarries. They are painted pale shades of pink, blue, green and tan. In the grassy yards grow shady trees, pink and white oleander and fuchsia-colored bougainvillea, a bushy plant with sweet-pea-shaped blossoms.

Saudi Arabian oil reaches the outside world by tankers and also through a 1,068-mile pipeline system completed in 1950 after three and a half years of work. It's known as Tapline, which is short for Trans-Arabian Pipe Line. Tapline carries oil from the Persian Gulf oil fields to Sidon in Lebanon, on the Mediterranean Sea. It crosses over yellow sand and black rocklands and fertile green valleys in Jordan, Syria and Lebanon. Through it, five big pump stations can move about 475,000 barrels of crude oil every day.

The oil is stored in huge tanks on a Sidon hillside overlooking the deep-blue waters of the Mediterranean. From the tanks it goes by underwater hoses to oil tankers anchored offshore.

Nearly 8,500 Saudi Arabs help produce this oil, which flows up through the wells at the rate of about 7,000,000 barrels a day. Yearly, Saudi Arabia earns over $2,000,000,000 from the operations of Aramco, which is short for Arabian American Oil Company. The company gets less money from the enterprise than Saudi Arabia.

Oil experts say there are over a hundred billion barrels of oil deep down under the country's scorching desert sands. Other oil companies operate in Saudi Arabia.

Saudi profits from the booming oil industry have made it possible for other modern businesses to thrive. The Saudis are a smart and eager people, and many of them have become skilled technicians, farmers and businessmen. They are in all sorts of trades, such as manufacturing cement, selling and repairing automobiles, freezing foods, generating electricity, building homes, and lots of others.

You can see why the sale of air conditioners is profitable. In this tropical country noon temperature in the desert sometimes reaches 130 degrees Fahrenheit!

The sun and the wind play the leading roles in Saudi weather. Say "May, June and July" to a Saudi and he's likely to say, "Oh, you mean the *shamal* season." A shamal is a sandstorm. In Arabic, shamal means north, and the sand is blown by a strong north wind. Sometimes a shamal will last for many days. The 50-mile-an-hour wind picks up the fine desert sand and blows it up and down and sideways all at the same time. It's a blizzard of sand that often hides the sun.

If you were out during a shamal, you would wear sunglasses and keep your mouth shut. When the wind-driven sand hits your face, it feels like hundreds of little pins stabbing at you. All mothers are glad when the shamal season is over, because there's no way of keeping the extra-fine sand from getting into the house. They have to dust all the time.

The sun shines almost every day of the year in Saudi Arabia. The white, yellow and red sands that cover most of the country reflect its bright rays. Most people wear sunglasses whenever they are outdoors.

Water is scarce. There are no lakes and rivers. There are many *wadis*, dry river beds, in the desert. When occasionally rains fall in torrents, the wadis fill up. But only temporarily. Then they look like lakes and rivers. The rest of the time they are beds of sand and gravel.

WADI

The Arabic language shows how the people feel about their weather. Men who live in cooler countries speak of good news as "heart-warming." But when the Arabs want to describe good news, they call it *akhbar tubarrid al qalb*, which means "heart-cooling."

Saudi Arabia's seasons correspond with those in the United States, but the difference between seasons in the desert country isn't as great. The hottest time of the year in Saudi Arabia is from May to September. Then the mercury sometimes tries to force its way out of the top of the thermometer. That's when you want to head for the swimming pool.

However, it would be a mistake to think that it's always hot in Saudi Arabia. You couldn't ask for more wonderful weather than the winter months bring. The temperature ranges from 45 degrees to 80 degrees. Your mother would be sure you had a sweater on if you were out playing after supper during the winter months.

Some Saudi boys wear an *aba* in cool weather. Aba is a word that frequently turns up in American crossword puzzles. It means a sleeveless cloak, usually brown. It's often made of camel hair.

Let's look at what else Hassan ibn Uthman wears. Hassan is a boy who lives with his family near al-Khobar.

Hassan's long white shirt is called a *thobe*. It runs from his neck all the way down to his ankles. On the top of his head, he wears a *gah-fiyah*, a little skullcap, that looks very much like the beanies some American children wear. A *gah-fiyah* can be plain or made from beautifully embroidered cloth. White is a favorite color for these caps.

46

When Hassan goes to the mosque with his father or visits friends or relatives, he also wears a *ghutra* and an *igal*. A *ghutra* is a square-shaped cloth draped on top of the *gah-fiyah*. Usually, but not always, a city Arab wears a white *ghutra* while a Bedouin prefers a red and white checkered one. The *igal* is a black cord that holds the *ghutra* in place. The *igal* is as thick as a heavy rope. It's wrapped around the head twice.

Some Saudi Arabs like young Hassan prefer sandals to shoes. They're much more comfortable in a hot climate and they're also better for walking on sand. Sandals are the oldest kind of shoes worn by man.

Hassan and his father remove their shoes when they enter their home as well as when they go into the mosque. When seated with their sandals on, they're careful not to let the soles show. It's considered very rude in Saudi Arabia to sit in a position so that the soles of your sandals can be seen.

Hassan has an eleven-year-old sister named Karima. She wears a long black dress trimmed with gold cloth. Like most Saudi Arab girls her age, she puts a veil over her face when she goes out in the street. The customs of Arabia call for young girls and women to cover their faces in public.

Most of the time boys like Hassan go out in public with their fathers, and girls like Karima with their mothers. Men and women don't gather together in public.

Hassan's full name, Hassan ibn Uthman, means Hassan, son of Uthman. Some Saudi Arabs don't use family names. Instead they identify themselves by giving their first name and then their father's first name. Uthman is the first name of Hassan's father. Hassan's sister's name, Karima, means "kind and generous." Her full name, Karima bint Uthman, means Karima, daughter of Uthman.

To avoid confusion, Saudis add their grandfather's and great-grandfather's names. Hassan calls himself Hassan ibn Uthman ibn Abdullah ibn Nasri. His grandfather's name was Abdullah. His great-grandfather's name was Nasri.

The children live with their mother and father on the outskirts of al-Khobar. Hassan's father has just built a new house there. He owns a large store in the suq, where he sells foreign cars. Uthman makes a good living. He used to work at the oil refinery at Ras Tanura. Like quite a number of Saudis, he saved his money until he had enough to go into business for himself.

Hassan's and Karima's new house, made of cement blocks, is laid out in Arab style. It's shaped like a rectangle with a wall six feet high on all sides so nobody can peek in from the street. Within this enclosure, the living quarters are shaped like an L. The remaining section is an open-air courtyard. The street entrances lead into the *majlis*, or living room. The floor of this room is covered with beautiful Oriental rugs. The children's father bought them on a trip to Iran, across the Persian Gulf.

The children's mother is an excellent cook. With the help of Karima, who is learning how to cook, she prepares wonderful meals for the family. You and other guests are expected today, so she and Karima are busy in the kitchen. The Saudi families are hospitable to visitors, whether relatives, friends or total strangers. They are known the world over for friendliness and generosity.

Today is a special time for feasting and merriment. It is Id al-Adha, the tenth day of the holy month in which pilgrimages are made, and is celebrated much as our Thanksgiving is. Families like to get together for it.

The other guests expected this afternoon are Bedouin relatives, an aunt and uncle and their son, Ibrahim. Ibrahim is Arabic for Abraham. Hassan is especially excited about Ibrahim's visit because both boys are the same age, ten years old. They haven't seen each other for some time and have much to talk about.

Sulaiman gives Uthman a warm handshake. They exchange greetings in the Arab manner, holding right hands until the greetings have been completed.

Cousin Ibrahim runs to greet Hassan. He says, "*As-salaam alaykum,*" which, as you know, means "Peace be upon you." Hassan starts off the conversation by telling Ibrahim about a soccer game he saw in Dammam a few days ago. Soccer is the most popular sport in Saudi Arabia. Saudi boys are real champions, and Hassan says he is going to be a team captain when he's older. Hassan also likes volleyball and tug-of-war. When he was younger, he used to enjoy playing "Button, button, who's got the button?" but now he thinks he's too old for that.

Hassan is interested in hearing about Ibrahim's excited plans to move into the city, but he doesn't really approve of them. Many Bedouins like Ibrahim's family are now settling in the cities. Nevertheless, Hassan thinks Ibrahim's present life in the desert, sleeping in different places, is a much more exciting way to live. He tells Ibrahim that once he has to go to school every day, he will change his mind about the city. The schools that young Arab boys and girls in towns attend are not much different from yours. The school buildings are usually no more than two stories high and each classroom has a big blackboard across one side of the wall. The pupils sit on chairs at little tables which serve as their desks. The subjects they study are like yours, too— geography, history, arithmetic, religion, and, while you study English, they study Arabic.

The Bedouin boys and girls, of course, have a freer life. The fathers tutor the boys in all the different subjects and the mothers teach the girls.

Hassan hears his mother calling. She tells him coffee is ready. Hassan goes into the kitchen and brings the big copper urn back into the majlis. The coffee urn has a long neck, filled with straw to filter the coffee. The coffee is sipped from little cups which have no handles, like the cups the Chinese use. Tea is also served. The teacups, made of glass, have handles. The tea is very sweet. The coffee is burning hot and spiced with cardamom seed. It

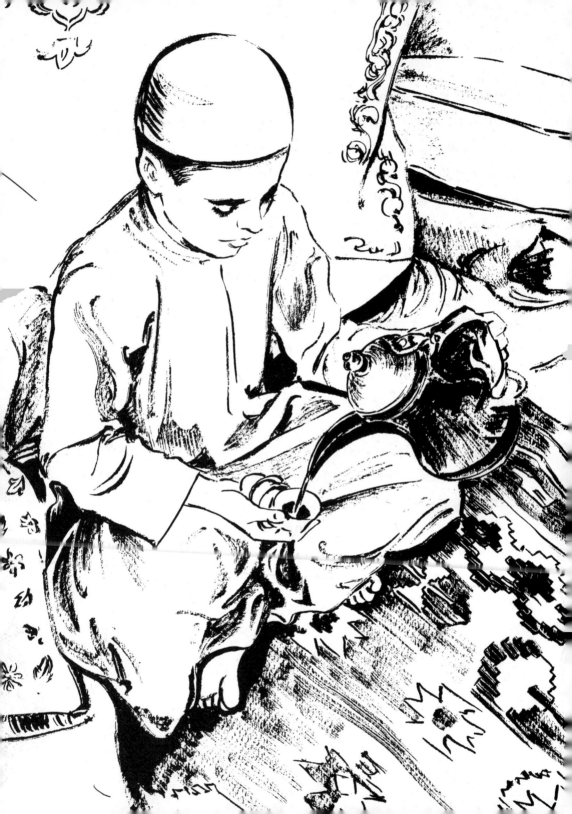

tastes a bit like liquid ginger. Hassan keeps filling the cups until the guests place their hands over the top and say *Bass*. This means enough, or no more. Serving coffee and tea is a gesture of welcome in any Arab house, tent or office.

Now the guests are ready to eat. Tonight they are all relatives, and you are special, so everybody sits down together, but usually when strangers are entertained, the women don't eat with the men. Uppermost in Uthman's mind is the comfort of his guests. He hardly sits down to the table at all, so busy is he, making sure his guests have plenty to eat.

The table is loaded. The main dish, one of the most popular in Saudi Arabia, is roast lamb with rice. The rice is deliciously flavored with almonds and raisins. Along with the main dish come heaping bowls of tomatoes, boiled beans, potatoes and carrots. Tonight these vegetables are fresh, but very often Arabs living in town will use canned or frozen foods. Uthman explains to you that in his father's house food used to be served in large platters placed on the floor, while all the diners sat on cushions. You think that might be fun, but Uthman's family prefers their table and chairs when eating.

After you have stuffed yourself at Uthman's urging, you wish you had saved more room for dessert. It's very fancy, a honey-covered pastry, made especially for this festive occasion. On ordinary nights the family would eat fruit for dessert, oranges or apples, or bananas or dates. Karima and her mother spent hours in the kitchen preparing the specialty you have tonight.

After the meal, coffee is served again while a burner of incense is passed around to each guest to inhale the fumes. You find the aroma very pleasant. The incense is a sign that the party is over. The guests usually depart after its burning. Hassan, Karima and their parents escort Ibrahim and his parents to the gate. Promises are made to get together soon again.

Before they leave, you hear Ibrahim and his mother and father say, "*Ashkurakum*," which means, "Thank you." Hassan and his family say, "*Fi aman allah*," which means "Go in the care of God."

Perhaps you would like to say the same to Hassan and Karima.

Word	Pronunciation		
Abd al-Aziz ibn Abd al-Rahman	*Ab*-dul az-*zeez* ibn Abd al-Rah-*maan*	Kayf haalak	Kaif haal-ak
Al Faisal Al Saud	al-*Fai*-sal al Sa-*oud*	La ilaha illa Allah	Laa il-*laa*-ha *il*-la *Al*-laah
Abqaiq	Ab-*cake*		
Abu Zaid al-Hilali	*A*-boo-zaid al-Hil-al-ee		
Ahlan wa sahlan	*Ah*-lan wa *sah*-lan	majlis	*maj*-lis
ain	ain	masjid	*mas*-jid
akhbar tubarrid al qalb	ak-*baar* to-*bar*-rid al gelb	Mohammed	Mo-*ham*-med
		meuzzin	moo-*ez*-zin
al-Khobar	al-Ko-bar	Muharram	Mu-*har*-ram
al Madinah al-Munawwarah	al-ma-*dee*-nah al-Mon-*naw*-a-rah		
		Qatar	*gut*-ter
As-salaam alaykum	As-sa-*laam* a-*lai*-kum	qidd	gid
		qirsh	gursh
barwag	*bar*-wag		
		Rabi' al-Awwal	*Ra*-bee al-*Aw*-wal
Dammam	Dam-*maam*	Rabi' al-Thani	*Ra*-bee a-*Thaa*-ni
dhanun	dah-*noon*	Rajab	*Raj*-ab
Dhahran	*Dah*-ran	rak	rack
Dhu al-Hijjah	Dool *Hid*-jah	Ramadhan	Rah-mah-*dan*
Dhu al-Qa'dah	Dool *Gaa*-dah	Ras Tanura	Ras Ta-*noo*-rah
Dhufar	*Do*-far	Riyadh	Ri-*yaad*
		riyal	ri-*yal*
gah-fiyah	gah-*fee*-ya	Rub al-Khali	Rube al *Ka*-li
ghutra	*gut*-rah		
		Safar	*Sa*-far
hamdh	hamdh	sayyafi	*sai*-a-fee
hamur	hah-*moor*	Sha'ban	Sha-*ban*
Hassan ibn Uthman	*Hass*-an ibn Uth-*man*	shamal	sha-*mal*
hawdaj	*how*-daj	Shawwal	Sha-*waal*
Hofuf	Ho-*foof*	Sulaiman	Soo-lay-*maan*
		suq	sook
igal	ee-*gaal*		
		Tayib, ashkurak	*Tai*-yib, ash-*koo*-rak
Jiddah	*Jid*-dah	thobe	thoab
Jumada al-Akhirah	Ju-*mad* al-A-*ki*-ra		
Jumada al-Ula	Ju-*mad* al-*Ou*-lah	Wa-alaykum as-salaam	Wa-a-*lai*-kum as-sa-*laam*
kanad	kan-*ad*	wadis	*wa*-dees
Karima	ka-*ree*-mah		
		zahra hamra	*zah*-rah *ham*-rah

* Italics indicate accent. Where no syllable is italicized the stress is equal.

SAY IT IN ARABIC

English	Hello	English	Good-bye
Arabic	Marhaba	Arabic	Fi aman allah
Pronunciation	*Mar*-hah-bah	Pronunciation	Fee a-*man* al-*laah*
English	Please	English	Thank you
Arabic	Min fadlak	Arabic	Ashkurakum
Pronunciation	Min *fadd*-lak	Pronunciation	Ash-*koor*-kum
	English	We are friends	
	Arabic	Nahnu asdigaa	
	Pronunciation	*Nah*-nu uss-dee-*gaa*	

SOME IMPORTANT DATES IN SAUDI ARABIAN HISTORY

570 — Birth of Mohammed at Mecca

622 — Founding of Islam

1880 — Birth of King Ibn Saud at Riyadh

1902 — Capture of Riyadh by Ibn Saud and his followers

1905 — Birth of present king of Saudi Arabia, King Faisal

1926 — Ibn Saud became king of the areas of Saudi Arabia he had conquered

1932 — The final step in the creation of a modern state was taken and the area was named The Kingdom of Saudi Arabia

1933 — The signing of the oil concession agreement with the Americans

1938 — The discovery of oil in Saudi Arabia

1953 — Death of King Ibn Saud

1953 — Prince Saud proclaimed King and Prince Faisal named Crown Prince

1964 — Faisal crowned King

INDEX

Aden, 8
Algeria, 12
animals, 28-32
Arabian American Oil Company, 42
Arabian horse, 28, 31
Arabian Peninsula, 7, 13
Arabic, 12, 13, 24, 25, 43, 45, 54, 60
Arabs, ancient, contributions of, 13, 14
Asia, 7, 13, 30
Atlantic Ocean, 12

Bedouins, 27-30, 33, 35, 39, 51, 53

Cairo, 13
calendar, 17
camels, 7, 28-30
cities
    Abqaiq, 40; al-Khobar, 26, 50; Dammam, 20; Dhahran, 8, 39; Hofuf, 22; Jiddah, 9, 19, 20; Mecca, 16, 18-20; Ras Tanura, 40, 50; Riyadh, 20
climate, 42-45
clothes, 45-49
crafts, 23, 24
currency, 26
customs, 48-50, 55-57

date palms, 33-35
desert, 13, 27-30, 33, 35, 39
Dhufar, 8

East Africa, 12
education, 55

farming, 12
fishing, 23
folklore, 28
food, 56-59

games, 52
government, 10, 12, 22, 56

holidays, 16, 51
houses, 40, 51

Indian Ocean, 7, 12, 14
Iraq, 8

Jordan, 8, 40

Kuwait, 8

Lebanon, 13, 40
locusts, 33

Mediterranean Sea, 42
Middle East, 13
Mohammed, 16, 18
Morocco, 12
mountains, 8
Muscat, 8

Nile River, 13

oases, 21, 33
oil, 12, 13, 35-42, 50
Oman, 8

pearl-diving, 24
Persian (Arabian) Gulf, 7-9, 20, 23, 26, 39
plants, 35, 40

Qatar, 8

Red Sea, 7, 9
religion, 15-20
Rub al-Khali, 39

Saud, King Ibn, 10, 11, 36
    sons of, 11
suq, 23
Syria, 40

transportation, 20, 22

United States, 8

water, 44

Yemen, 8